To Tsehai,
you are a blessing
in my life.

May the glory
Shine upon you

Isa. 60:1

With love

Hirut

BROKEN TO SHINE

BROKEN TO SHINE

HIRUT WOLDE THOMPSON

Story Terrace

Text Lusine Khachatryan, on behalf of StoryTerrace

Interior Design StoryTerrace

Cover Design LPS Marketing Designs, LLC

Copyright © Hirut Wolde Thompson

ISBN 978-0-578-29644-9

Library of Congress Control Number 2022909742

First Print December 2022

StoryTerrace

www.StoryTerrace.com

For more information contact:

hirut14@verizon.net

DEDICATIONS

In loving memory of my beloved parents, Wolde Woldemariam and Wuleta Geremu, who are my examples of strength, courage, and perseverance, as well as my big sister/mentor Pamela Dodson and mother/mentor Doris Pugh, who were the backbone of my journey into adulthood.

To my siblings: Merkebu, Etenesh, Feseha and Sammy, you are the core of my journey. Growing up with you has been the best part of my life. To my extended siblings in Ethiopia, although I didn't grow up with you, we are connected through our mother's love and legacy for the love of family.

ACKNOWLEDGMENTS

I am grateful to my Lord and Savior, Jesus Christ, who lovingly used my life to write a story that has the power to change lives and bring healing to that little girl, young lady, and woman who is broken through life and give her the power to shine to show His glory.

To my best friend of 38 years and husband of 31 years, Anthony Thompson, who always goes out of his way to elevate me as his queen and respect me as his wife and best friend. This book project is possible because he believed that **I CAN**.

To my beautiful children, Feshaun and Sasha Thompson, my blessings from God, my saving grace, you brought joy and fulfillment to my life.

Pastor Bernard Fuller and First Lady Fuller, thank you for believing in me and providing me with the spiritual guidance that I needed throughout my journey.

Thank you, Rachael Turner, Yolanda Dudley, and Lori Dixon. Not knowing what God challenged me to do, you spoke life into the vision that I was afraid to execute.

Paula Benjamin and Cassandra Hall, my prayer warriors, you invested hours of your day to review my work from cover to cover and provided me with authentic feedback.

Thank you, Monica Fortune, Ruth Hopkins, Roberta Edwards for being the extra eyes and ears that I needed and for the many conversations we shared as we took walks. Sandra Thompson and Aunt Vernice Thompson, for being my faithful cheerleaders.

Evangeline (Barbara) Crawford, my childhood bestie, through you I met the love of my life. Rene Johnson, you took me under your wings at the age of 18 and mentored me into womanhood. I love and appreciate you both for being part of my journey.

I am also super grateful for my many girlfriends for trusting me with their friendships, encouraging me to pursue my dreams, and allowing me to share the good and the bad of my life's journey without judgment.

Finally, I want to extend my gratitude to all the individuals that will be blessed by God's story through my journey. It is my prayer and hope that as you read *Broken To Shine*, you will find a breakthrough and the courage to be a light for others to see.

ABOUT THE AUTHOR

Hirut Thompson is a faithful follower of Jesus Christ and is passionate about the journey that God has determined for her life. She is a devoted wife, mother of two beautiful daughters, and a mentor for young women in her community. Hirut's book, *Broken To Shine*, is a testament to how God has guided her throughout her life and how she endured and overcame many obstacles while still shining for God to be seen through her.

Many aspects of Hirut's life resemble that of many others. Nevertheless, what defines her story is her unique response to life's circumstances and her faith in God to embrace and push through with perseverance. Being surrounded by the love of her best friend and husband of 31 years, Anthony (Tony), and her two adopted children, Feshaun and Sasha, allows her to shine through her brokenness.

Through her experiences, Hirut was shaped to foster her ministry of mentoring young ladies and women and providing them with the tools needed for a faithful walk in Christ and to live a life free from bondage, fear, and doubt. Thus, her goal for *Broken To Shine* is to encourage phenomenal women to choose to let God's unfailing love, grace, and mercy shine through them for others to see.

Hirut and Tony have been faithful members of New Song Bible Fellowship Church in Lanham, MD spanning more than 30 years, where they raised both of their daughters and currently serve in various lay leadership roles. In 2020, the couple embarked on the new season of their journey as empty nesters and grandparents to their beautiful Shih Tzu/Yorkie dog, Mango.

Hirut desires to please God with every part of who she is and to make a positive impact on those around her. Her determination becomes even more powerful knowing that God keeps His promise: "Being confident of this very thing, that He who has begun a good work in you will complete it until the day of Jesus Christ." Philippians 1:6.

CONTENTS

BROKEN TO SHINE

HIRUT WOLDE THOMPSON

StoryTerrace

FOREWORD

"Hirut Thompson has been my best friend for approximately 38 years and my wife and lifelong partner for 31 years. I have been blessed to walk part of this journey alongside her. She has been a wonderful wife and mother. Through all the storms that life has brought her way, she has triumphed through her faith in God.

"God has made the difference in her life and in our marriage. When God placed the idea to write this book in her spirit, there were so many obstacles in the way that delayed this project. I am so excited that she persevered, and now we have seen this book come to fruition. Our hopes and prayers are that this book will be a blessing and an encouragement to those who read it."

Anthony Thompson, Husband

"From a wonderful unique woman comes a powerful unique story. Hirut Thompson's life is a testimony to God's grace and faithfulness. It has been a joy and an honor to be her pastor for over 30 years now. Her life has demonstrated the love and power of God and the fact that He can be trusted. In her humble and articulate way, Hirut tells her life story. I am confident you will be blessed and that God will use this book to inspire many as Hirut's life has inspired me."

Dr. Bernard T. Fuller, Senior Pastor
New Song Bible Fellowship Church
Lanham, Maryland

"When I think of Hirut, I think of the words courage and friendship (which is actually one of the meanings of her name). Her love for God and her love for people have been a theme in her life for as long as I have known her. We have been prayer partners for over 20 years and have seen God answer so many of our prayers. I always looked forward to our Tuesday night prayer times. We have witnessed God's power and faithfulness working in our lives.

"Hirut writing this book, *Broken To Shine*, speaks volumes to how she is ministering to others who are going through various trials and how they can overcome through faith and trust in God. Diamonds aren't shiny and perfectly shaped from the beginning. They are found in dirt and sand as rocks; they are broken and crushed and have to go through a refining process. Only 20% of selected diamonds can be polished. This reminds me of how this book depicts Hirut's life. Her resilience, faith, and courage are the result of her refining process, and God is polishing her life to shine for the world to see His glory!"

Cassandra Hall, Prayer Partner

OVERVIEW

When we walk in our purpose and follow our calling, everything in life becomes possible. No journey is too difficult. In our tears, there is joy. In our trials, there is triumph. When we walk in our purpose, the answers to all of life's questions become illuminated, and we find life amid death. My name is Hirut Wolde Thompson, and this is the story of my journey, crafted and designed by God, with experiences that have been stepping stones to greatness and a model to each person I encounter.

As you read this book, regardless of the challenges that life has and will bring your way, my heart's desire is that you will experience the power and love of God, understand your purpose, and shine so others can see God through you.

CHAPTER 1

THROUGH MY FATHER'S EYES

Created on Purpose for His Purpose

My life's journey began on July 14, 1966, when I was born to the late Wolde Woldemariam and Wuleta Geremu in beautiful Addis Ababa, the capital city of Ethiopia. Born into a family of high priests and generals, I was the second of four children to my parents. Looking back at my world and all that came with it, I have no doubt or questions about my purpose. I have experienced every emotion known to man: Some I was born with, others I learned, and some were created by the choices I made.

I can remember as early as three or four years old the changes that affected our family unit as I knew it. Our parents did all they could to create a happy home for my siblings and me. My father worked to provide for our family, and my mother stayed home to raise us. When my dad's work took him away from our home often, I had a difficult time adjusting to his absence. It became clear to me that our family dynamic was changing. Our "normal" was no longer normal. Although I loved both of my parents, I was a daddy's girl, and his absences caused me great sorrow. As a result, my heart often felt dark and gloomy, but I didn't know how to express what I was feeling. Therefore, I internalized my thoughts while I learned to manage my emotions, keep hope alive, and trust the unknown. God was evident in my situation, as I often experienced a ray of bright sunshine in the depths of my soul, and the peace of God shined through every circumstance that I encountered.

Although I couldn't articulate what was going on within me, nor did I understand what was taking place, His purpose was embedded in my soul when He created me to display His love, compassion, and power for the world to see and experience.

I grew up in a culture where children did not have a voice. You did what you were told and spoke only when you were spoken to. You did not dare ask questions, especially about adult matters. But my dad's absence was so real to me even at that young age. After a while, I slowly lost hope of seeing him, and the unfulfilled desire of living in a home with two parents became my painful reality. The spirit of darkness took up residence in my heart, where innocent love and hope had once lived.

Overcome by loneliness and rejection, I began to create stories of how my dad must have died in a horrible accident somewhere in the world. It was the only way I could explain his prolonged absence. Even as a child, I refused to accept the idea that my dad had gone away because he didn't love or want us. Even though my mind struggled with not having my dad and with the possibility of not seeing him again, my heart was committed to the hope of reuniting with him.

Life Changes, but God Remains the Same

My earthly father had been given by God a spirit to accept challenges, live with courage, and smile in the face of many adversities. As he did what was necessary to provide for our family, he held many jobs, but the one that had a big impact on our lives was his job at the Embassy of Ghana. Several years into his employment, his pleasant disposition and strong work ethic endeared him to his boss, who invited him to his deployment in New York City. Dad could not let this opportunity go. As difficult as it was for him to leave his family, he courageously moved to the United States to work for an unknown period. Though he planned to come home to check on us, his visits made life even more bittersweet. My happiness at seeing him was short-lived because I knew he would have to leave, and I would miss him all over again. The long-term impact of separation on me was enormous, even into adulthood. As a child, I began to internalize the separation as abandonment and wondered *what is wrong with me. Why is he not coming home?* Without understanding it, fear and loneliness found a place in my heart.

My dad was the first love and security I knew. His absence also caused despair in my heart that I couldn't shake, and I began to digress in life. I literally could not distinguish my right hand from my left. I got into trouble for writing and eating with the wrong hand. Learning to keep my struggles to myself, I cried silently, and no one knew. Sometimes my dad sent suitcases of goodies home, which helped put a smile on my face and reminded me that he had not forgotten about me. However, it did not ease the emptiness or replace his hugs. As far as others were concerned, we were living a privileged life. Some may have thought the fancy outfits, shoes, toys, and books were worth having a father living abroad. They were not, and they did not answer the questions of what we had done wrong. Why we didn't have both our parents was a constant source of doubt in my young mind.

Even though my mom tried maintaining a sense of security, she too began experiencing the power of abandonment and loneliness. As a young girl, I did not understand that my parents' marriage was arranged due to the politics of their family dynamics and that they had not married for love. Emotional distress and physical breakdown were inevitable as my mom dealt with the challenges of trying to be both a mom and a dad. As the middle child, I often felt her attention diverted to my little sister or older brother, who was always getting into trouble. I buried my sorrow and made the best of my little life while endlessly waiting for my daddy to return.

Unfortunately, because she struggled with life and felt hopeless, my mom made decisions that impacted her marriage to our dad. In his absence, the spirit of infidelity entered our home. Our once joy-filled, two-parent house became a place of sadness, uncertainty, and emotional isolation. While away, my father learned of my mom's situation and made an emergency trip home to quickly move my siblings and me several hours outside of Addis Ababa to live with his relatives in Kembata, Durame. This was the sad reality of my parents' marriage ending. Due to the nature of their abrupt separation and the pain between them, my mom was forbidden from and threatened about making any attempts to find us. Something was going on, but we didn't know what it was, how long it would last, and why we were there. *I was too young to know the truth, but I wasn't too young to feel the pain.* The sudden change from the city to the country, the separation from my parents, and being forced to learn a different language and culture made for an incredibly challenging life. It validated the loneliness and abandonment I'd felt as a child.

Settling Into My New Normal

Change was difficult for me to handle, especially at seven years old. Initially, my dad was with us, so I was not as bothered that we were in an unfamiliar place with relatives we did not know, but the day he left is a memory etched in my mind. I remember him kissing us and saying goodbye. When his car pulled away, I stood at the fence and couldn't stop crying. I was told he had gone to buy a new dress for me, and he'd be back soon, but deep inside,

I knew it wasn't true. He'd gone away before, so I knew this was no different. As the sun set, "Where is my daddy?" I asked. "Where is my dress?" The following day, I waited for him in the same place until the sky grew dark again. Sometimes I was spanked for not going inside, not eating, and not following instructions given by my aunt and uncle. A day became a week; a week became a month. A month turned into six years of emotional, mental, and physical pain as my spirit grew weary and loneliness began to cloud my heart again.

The church became my only place of hope, peace, and comfort as I began to desire the things of God. While my siblings had fun on Saturday afternoons, I began my preparations for Sunday services by fixing snacks as an offering to the nuns and priests. Early on Sunday mornings, I made my way to church, climbing the hills and going through the valleys in pain and in fear of wild animals. I pressed forward because all along, God was walking with me. In my pain and sorrow, God was pointing me to Him.

REFLECTIONS

I was too young to know the truth, but I wasn't too young to feel the pain.

The sad scenario is that there are so many children who grow up in emotional pain and become damaged boys and girls with no sense of direction or hope. I was one of those children, but the grace and mercy of God spared and protected me.

As a child, I never understood why I had to experience life as I did. Even now, as an adult, I still do not understand; but I learned to hold on to the hand of God, embrace His heart, and made a choice that *loneliness and silence would never speak for me and hide the beauty I represent in Christ*. As I searched for answers to my questions, God was sowing a seed in my heart that would protect me from the obstacles that would come my way. The pieces of the puzzle were coming together perfectly even then. The power of separation is stronger than most of us can imagine or manage. However, I've learned from my experiences that no age is too young to feel the pain of abandonment and rejection.

THOUGHTS FOR YOUR JOURNEY

A father's presence in his daughter's life is a remarkable experience for any child. In a similar manner, the absence of a father can, however, lead to unexplained challenges in life, such as unhealthy relationships. There is beauty and strength in a father's love that can lend an opportunity to change the unforeseen events of life and push you into greatness. For some, the lack of an earthly father's love can be painful and make you question your purpose and relationship with God. Be encouraged to know that what seems unknown to you is well known to God, your Heavenly Father. What are your unanticipated experiences in life that resulted from your father-daughter relationship or lack thereof? Take a moment to evaluate your life and share your testimony with someone who needs a breakthrough because God has a plan and purpose in it.

"For I know the thoughts that I think toward you, says the Lord, thoughts of peace and not of evil, to give you a future and a hope."

Jeremiah 29:11

"How precious also are your thoughts to me, O God! How great is the sum of them! If I should count them, they would be more in number than the sand; When I awake, I am still with you."

Psalm 139:17-18

Approximately three years old with my maternal grandparents and my mom

My siblings and I, photo taken to send to dad in USA

Approximately 4 years old

CHAPTER 2

A JOURNEY TRAVELED BY *FAITH*

The Unexpected New

Traveling from one state to another in Ethiopia to live with my dad's uncle, I found life as I knew it was very different. Not only did I lose the affection and presence of my dad, but the sudden relocation deprived me of my mom and what I had known to be home and family. Ethiopia is a country with many tribes that have their own culture and dialect. Moving meant learning a whole new way of life, a new language, and different foods; it meant becoming accustomed to yet another change.

Before leaving to return to America, my dad made certain we had everything we needed. He also provided his uncle with the finances to build a house for us. We were to live as we were accustomed to living. However, the fear of being left behind was an overwhelming experience that gripped my heart and emotions, but God in His sovereignty gave me the faith, even as a child, to choose to stand up and live up to the plans He had created for my life.

Ultimately, my dad's goal was to bring us to the United States, but until he could, his desire was for us to stay with his uncle, who was the town's elder and a high priest in the Orthodox church. He fought to keep us, not only because we were his nephew's children, but because keeping us came with benefits to the family, carried a huge status, and meant there was wealth to be had. His four children were a little older than us, and it was believed that they, along with his wife, would be a great help in raising us. With the demands of my great-uncle's role as the head priest, it was impossible for him to be present. Even though he often was not there and didn't know much about us, everything needed his stamp of approval. Even though his wife was a silent strength, she couldn't make any decisions pertaining to us; so, we were left to fend for ourselves..

Initially, we were a big deal and a show-and-tell for the family and the town, but soon, the honeymoon stage wore off, and we became like everyone else, fighting to survive. Growing up with our parents, we had workers doing everything for us. But in my new life, I found myself mopping the floors, helping in the kitchen, tending to the animals that were purchased for our use, cleaning the barn on my hands and knees, and working on the farm harvesting. Unfortunately, we were treated more like workers than like children. Imagine the confusion in my seven-year-old mind as I was overwhelmed with sadness and the feeling of abandonment from the love and attention that I had known in my precious formative years.

As time went on, my dad's siblings began fighting to take us from his uncle. My aunts felt they had the right to have us because we were their nieces and nephews. Sometimes, they even kidnapped us as we walked home from school. We were trapped in the middle of a tug-of-war. My siblings preferred my dad's uncle, but I felt closer to my aunts. They reminded me so much of my dad. I let them take me several times, but soon, the town's council became involved, and it was ruled that, by law, my dad's uncle would have us. Since he was one of the town's elders and the top Orthodox priest, everything worked in his favor. My dad was contacted, and while he never explained why, he confirmed their decision and felt we were better off with his uncle. Once my father confirmed his plans for us, my aunts eventually stopped trying because they knew the legal ramifications of their continued attempts.

Physical Scars Caused by Emotional Sorrows

During the back and forth, my young body was under so much stress that I began catching all kinds of infections, fevers, and sores. Some were contagious and affected the entire household. At one point, I caught a contagious virus with a fever that made everyone in the home so ill that we thought we'd lose my baby brother. I was not eating or resting properly, and my immune system was compromised at many levels. I was called "bad luck" and labeled as a child of the devil. I was extremely depressed and heard negative comments so often that I began to believe them.

I went to sleep crying and awoke in the same state, but no one was concerned if I was emotionally unwell or homesick. Every day, I wondered how I would make it through the day. Loneliness grew faster than I was growing, and for as long as I can remember, my childhood was spent in survival mode. I was hurting so badly inside that it was manifesting on the outside. I was accustomed to my mom giving us baths and changing us often, but now I would wake up wearing the same clothes I'd had on the day before. The house my father had financed was taken over by his uncle's children, and we found ourselves fighting for attention, food, and even for beds to sleep in.

During this time, I developed a little bump on my leg that itched. I was told that it was a bug bite that would heal if I didn't touch it. Unfortunately, it wasn't easy to deal with the itch. One scratch after another caused me to develop an open wound that grew into a physical problem that would affect me for a lifetime. It hurt so much that for many nights the pain kept me awake, and I could not find a comfortable position to sleep without the wound sticking to the blankets and sheets. I felt worthless and fearful, and I missed having a mom for comfort and guidance. I was teased and picked on at school, and the thought of facing the world for another day was unbearable.

During this time, my dad asked us to write him letters to keep him updated. He promised us that if we weren't doing well, he would come back and get us. Each time we wrote him letters, his uncle read them first and if they didn't reflect that we were doing well, he instructed us to rewrite them.

Although my dad's instructions were to take us directly to the hospital if we were ill, his uncle kept the money and instead found home remedies for the wound on my leg. I was treated with a plant-based concoction that I was allergic to. After a few homemade treatments, the bump grew so big it covered my entire leg. Eventually, they grew tired of trying to figure it out. I was told to wash it with soap and water, but the infection was so harsh that it had begun eating into the bone. It was so raw. It bled uncontrollably and constantly oozed pus. Imagine the embarrassment and shame I was carrying. To hide it, I tied a scarf over it or wore pants and socks, which would stick to it and become more painful to remove at night. I was shunned by my classmates, and the neighborhood children didn't want to play with me. To save my siblings from the embarrassment, I stayed inside while they played all day. To keep my mind busy and pass the time, I began to work around the house, helping with household chores.

I knew my aunt wanted to help, but to speak up would have been dishonorable to her husband. She never had the freedom to openly care, but she silently and secretly did everything she could to comfort me. Knowing that nights were more challenging for me, she would sit by my bedside and massage every part of my body that ached while tears streamed down from her eyes. I knew she was praying for me because when she was around, I felt the presence of peace and fulfillment. She allowed me to cry and sleep on her shoulder. My great-uncle did not want to bring attention to the difficulty I was having and made sure everything was kept light and hush. If word reached my dad that any of us were not doing well, it could stop the benefits they were receiving to care for us. My aunt kept me near her, regardless of the odor and grossness of my wound. She washed me with her bare hands because she believed that her touch would bring me comfort, and it did. The painful sore stayed on my leg for six years, and one day I woke up to find that I had developed maggots (baby flies) that were eating my flesh.

When the maggots appeared, I started to think about dying. In fact, I felt like life was over for me. I was supposed to be clean and have the best shoes and clothes. I could not understand why this was happening. "Oh, somebody stinks!" the kids around me would say. Even adults who saw my leg shunned me because it looked gross, and the infection was so bad that I carried a stench that no human should have. I was disgusted by my own body as blood and pus oozed out of my leg. And while others could walk away from it, I had to live with it. Being motherless suddenly became such a painful reality, and my emotions were at an all-time low. Abandonment and separation were clearly leading me to anger. I started thinking about hanging myself, but I was too short to reach anything. I thought about drowning in the lake behind the house where we lived, but I was too scared.

Unfortunately, I began to believe the voice of satan, and my self-confidence started breaking down. I told myself that I was not worthy and that God did not exist. After all, my parents didn't want anything to do with me, so why should anybody else? I was struggling with questions of why I existed and what my purpose was. It was then that I realized that although I was broken and hurting, feeling so worthless and not capable of living without my parents in the condition I was in, God softened my little heart to love myself despite my circumstances. Even though I did not know God and did not understand the magnitude of His love for me, I began to speak with Him as if He was one of my imaginary friends it was safe to open up to. I boldly expressed to Him that I wanted to die. I did not know what was wrong with me, but I knew that God heard me and could help me push through this fearful season of life.

Days later, my brother outsmarted my great-uncle by writing two letters instead of just one. In the first letter, he told the usual lie about us being fine, and in the second, he wrote a cry for help. My brother gave the first letter to him and found a way to mail the second letter himself.

When the letter finally reached my dad, he immediately got on a plane. No one knew he was coming home; therefore, there hadn't been any preparation. When the car drove up with a cloud of dust behind it, the neighbor's kids started screaming, "Wolde is home!" Because it had been some time since he'd been back to the town he grew up in, his arrival was a big deal to the community. Everyone was out to witness his presence. The family was scrambled and working in different areas of the farm. My dad had left us with everything we needed, but upon his return, we didn't even have a pair of shoes. I had one pair of rubber jelly sandals, which I couldn't wear on the farm because they were so hot that they burned and blistered my feet. All our clothes were taken either by my great-uncle's children or by the neighborhood kids. Nothing my father had sent was reaching us. I never knew what happened to those things, and neither did my dad.

I remember this experience like it was yesterday. As the car made its way down the road, the adults were yelling, "Gather the kids. Clean them up," but I was so embarrassed that I hid. My whole childhood, I convinced myself that Dad wasn't alive. If he had been, he would have come back for my siblings and me. As happy as he was to see my siblings, he asked, "Where's my daughter? I was told she has been sick." As much as I had dreamed of seeing him, I knew I was dirty and smelly, and my hair was matted in place. I didn't believe he would still have the same love for me. When they found me, I was so embarrassed to be in his presence, I wouldn't look up. When I finally did, tears were coming out of every part of my dad's face. "Let's go!" he said. As they were slaughtering a bull and chickens for a big celebration, my dad said, "Thank you for mistreating my children who I trusted you with." At that very moment, I saw the work of God in my life so clearly. Only one week after I'd spoken to Him, my dad had arrived.

Wearing My Scars With Grace

Emotional, physical, and spiritual pain have been part of who I am for as long as I can remember, but as life has dragged me from one sad event to another, God has always granted me the grace to soar through the pain and rise above to experience praise. I believe seasons and stages of life are appointed before our existence. Some seasons are so overwhelming that we wish to deny them, swap them, abandon them, or give them back. But the reality of life is that they are ours to own. Not walking through them as we should causes the journey to be more challenging. Truly, what God has planned for us is specifically for us, and we must grab hold and endure the journey of our appointed seasons. Although we have no control over them, *how* we respond determines our destiny. For me, accepting the hands that were dealt for me and learning to honor God through it all are the keys to my victory.

REFLECTIONS

When we gather with family and friends, we love playing card games like Phase 10 or Uno, and I often find it so difficult to manage the cards dealt for me—not to mention the extra cards that I pick up from the deck along the way. Having what I call a bad hand and not being able to throw any cards out when it's my turn, it takes extra time for me to complete my move because I have difficulty managing what's in my hand. But win or lose, my goal is to always play the hand dealt to me and find enjoyment in the game.

For as long as I can remember, my life has been just like the cards in my hand. While some phases were more difficult than others, I learned to persevere and push through towards victory. Just like the card games, sometimes I win, and sometimes I lose, but that is part of the course. The goal is to finish the journey in a way that will bring honor to God and fulfill His plans for my life.

THOUGHTS FOR YOUR JOURNEY

Whether we plan it, or life appoints it for us, we must all journey through life. ***The attitude we carry throughout our journey determines the outcome of victory or defeat.*** On our path, sometimes we must take difficult roads while we also experience rewarding moments. Think about a moment in your life that was difficult or rewarding. What was your attitude and the outcome?

"Finally, brethren, whatever things are true, whatever things are noble, whatever things are just, whatever things are pure, whatever things are lovely, whatever things are of good report, if there is any virtue and if there is anything praiseworthy—meditate on these things."

Philippians 4:8

My siblings and godbrother with my dad

Tony and I sharing a meal during his visit to our home

Enjoying a glass of soda at a Safeway Christmas party with my mother-in-law

High school graduation day with my favorite principal, Mr. Boarman

My senior prom (1985) – dress designed by
Aunt Wreatha Anderson, a close family friend

Senior prom (1985) – my first formal date
with Tony

CHAPTER 3

A PRAYER ANSWERED

Understanding the Purpose of Prayer

P rayer is a form of authentic conversation one has with God. It's an opportunity when every human must share their heart's concerns with the hope of receiving an answer that will make a difference in their journey. *A prayer is a key to a breakthrough from life's bondage or from circumstances beyond one's control.* It is a conversation that you'll never have to question regarding whether it is heard and understood, one that will leave you fulfilled and encouraged, one that will teach you perseverance. Life is a journey that is bound to happen, and it is necessary for our growth and development. Therefore, understanding your source of help through the journey is a very important concept. Whether you are praying for salvation, direction, or deliverance for yourself or others, what a blessing it would be to engage with the Master of creation and the one who knows the beginning and end of your journey.

My desire to talk with God began after the very first traumatic experience of my little life, the separation from my mom and dad. Did I understand what was going on? No, but I always felt there was a God somewhere that I could call on for help. During that period, unfortunately, I was labeled as a problem child because I was often talking to myself. Little did they know I was never by myself. And eventually, when I was 18 years old, I made a public declaration for the Lord to become my Lord and Savior, and I never looked back. God hears my prayers and answers me in a special way. God has been and is my go-to in every circumstance that I face.

God Listens and Answers

Once we returned to Addis Ababa, my dad took me to one of the best hospitals in the city, where doctors cleaned my wound and gave me three different forms of antibiotics. Amazingly, God healed six years of infection in a single week. Doctors said if I had waited just two more weeks, I would have lost my leg. I knew it was true because it had become weaker to use, and the infection was beyond the surface. As a child, instead of playing with other children and enjoying my innocence, I grew up making plans for the unknown. I visualized myself using a wheelchair and often imagined wearing prostheses, but I thank God for the power of His healing. Although I am left to wear a scar, I am grateful to have two legs I can use to walk through the journey that God has appointed for me. I am a true miracle of God's healing power.

Soon after I received my treatment and my dad felt comfortable that my siblings and I were safe and in a better place, he returned to the United States to continue working and to prepare for our future. You see, it wasn't like the first time when he had disappeared before my eyes. This time, he promised he would come back for us soon. Until he returned, my siblings and I were to stay with his other uncle in the city, the one we'd grown up with. Even though my dad promised, I still had reservations. I didn't want to be left behind again, but I understood a little more now, and I accepted the fact that he had to go back to the United States. I also believed that if he had come back after all those years, he would come back again.

Not All Answers to Prayer Are Yes

As part of his preparations to move us to the United States to be with him, my dad felt it was important for us to have motherly support in the home, so he decided to get married again. During that time, my older brother was 15 years old, I was 13, my younger sister was 12, and my baby brother was 10—a lot to handle for my dad on his own. Of course, his uncle had much to do with identifying a young lady for my dad to marry. His uncle thought that the selected individual would be a good fit as a wife and a mother figure to my siblings and me. At that time, we had no clue she would eventually be our stepmom and move to the United States with us. Was that what I prayed for?

No! My prayer had always been for my parents to reunite and for us to be the family unit we had previously been. However, God had a different plan, which was beneficial to all.

When you live life right, the blessings and favor of God are immeasurable and amazing. The Ghana Embassy had been reassigned to Switzerland and sought to take my dad, but because of the wealth of opportunities in the United States and his vision of raising us in the land of many freedoms, my dad was willing to do anything to stay in the United States. Even if it meant taking the chance of facing trouble for breaking his contractual agreement to return home, he was willing to suffer the consequences. His agreement with the Ghana Embassy was for him to return to Ethiopia at the conclusion of his tour of duty unless he was reassigned with the current Ghana Ambassador. However, as a compromise, he'd been handed over to the Ethiopian Embassy in Washington, D.C., leaving it up to them to make the final decision to return or reassign him. Here was another answered prayer. Dad was blessed to be given an opportunity to work temporarily as a building superintendent and a chauffeur for the Ambassador of Ethiopia in exchange for room and board.

As time went on, he was able to find full-time work for an influential Jewish family. His great work ethic and cheerful disposition had endeared him to the family so much that during the military regime in Ethiopia, when it was difficult to receive visas, they were instrumental in helping my dad by sponsoring our whole family, including my dad's new wife, my stepmother, to move to the United States. In addition, Dad's connections back home helped complete the process with the American Embassy, allowing us to exit Ethiopia.

God Knows Best

The time had come for the wedding ceremony and preparations to move to the United States. For the first time, my sister and I were sent to the beauty salon to get our hair done for the wedding. Because of years of neglect, our once nurtured and groomed hair was now dry and matted to the point that it was beyond repair. The only option was to cut it short and start over again. Even though I really didn't understand all that was going on, the day of the wedding celebration was bittersweet for me. I can clearly remember asking God, "What happened to my mom? Will I ever see her again?" Despite years of separation, I had hoped and believed we would be reunited with my mom and dad, but that wasn't so. Suddenly, a sense of disappointment hovered over my soul, and I had a small doubt about prayers.

Looking back, I often wonder, if I'd had a mom, would I have experienced the hardships of life? Would my leg have been infected? Would I have been called the devil? I was angry that we had been abandoned, abused, and mistreated. The only one I thought would understand me was God, but now I was questioning that, too.

The unknown was once again staring at me head-on. But knowing that my dad would be with me and that I would no longer be a parentless child, I was released from the fear of abandonment. The pain from my six years of infection was gone, making it easier to accept our new journey to the United States to live with Daddy. In September 1979, my father returned to Ethiopia with five Permanent Residence (or Green) Cards, and at the conclusion of his wedding, he proudly escorted us to the United States to begin our new chapter of life.

REFLECTIONS

Dear Lord, thank you for choosing me for this journey called life. You fearfully and wonderfully created me and have given me the desire to be me. You have been with me since before I knew myself. You carried me through all the unknowns of life and gave me joy through every circumstance. You have healed my soul, mind, and body. I am so grateful and full of pride to be your daughter and servant.

THOUGHTS FOR YOUR JOURNEY

What areas of life have you sought God for? And what was the outcome of your conversation? I encourage you to share your testimony of answered prayers with someone and see how it will encourage them.

"Now this is the confidence that we have in Him, that if we ask anything according to His will, He hears us. And if we know that He hears us, whatever we ask, we know that we have the petitions we have asked of Him."

I John 5:14

Prayer with my church care group family

My Heartbeats, the Fruits of my Journey

My sister and me

CHAPTER 4

LIFE IN A NEW WORLD

My Own Coming to America!

My vision of the United States was different from what I found it to be. Just as the media portrays Ethiopia as a poverty-stricken, third-world country, my image of America from television programs and what I had heard was totally the opposite of reality. In my childlike mind, America was a place of milk and honey where there are no worries of missing a meal or sleep, where there are open possibilities to do what you want and be whom you want. I anticipated a life like the Jetsons', a country where you push a button and life happens for you, where a robot gives you your meal and cleans up after you. In the mornings, your closet opens with a push of a button, and your daily outfit is chosen for you.

However, when we landed in New York City, I was very confused. I could not believe we were in the United States. There were homeless people asleep on the streets of America, and there were panhandlers all around the airport. There was trash thrown in the streets, and as I looked around, there were all kinds of people. My first thought was, *Wow! What kind of place is this?* There were all races of people—I never knew America was a true melting pot with people from all around the world. I was so shocked and overwhelmed; I remember asking if we were in America yet. But I quickly realized life was no different here than in Ethiopia, except for better opportunities to learn, work, and live due to a wealthy economy. Oh my! That day, I learned about the difference between television and reality.

A few months into our relocation, my school transcripts arrived, and I started school. I was the only Ethiopian in a predominantly African American environment. Adjusting to a new culture wasn't easy, and it wasn't an option. In my mind, I was prepared not to let that experience beat what I grew up with. However, fear of rejection was replaying in the forefront of my mind as I was teased for my difficulties speaking English the American way and for being a foreigner from Africa, who, God forbid, was light-skinned and had good hair. Quickly, I realized that the same misconception and misunderstanding I'd had about America was what the children in America had about Ethiopia. I felt I had to find a way to help them understand that what they'd seen on TV was not really who we were as a country. I was determined not to allow the mean middle school children to break me down with their misunderstandings. Each day that I went to school, the children made sure I was aware that I didn't belong with them or in their school. ***But early on in life,***

I had decided that I was beautiful, I was important, and I mattered, if to no one else, to God.

As I entered middle school, I drew strength from the hardships of my childhood and pushed through to rise above all that came against me. With my young mind, I began to defend myself. I made the attempt to convince my peers that I had lived a good life. In Ethiopia, it's typical for a normal household to have workers who help with raising children, cooking, and doing typical household chores. I remember sharing that with the children at school to prove to them that I came from a family who had class. I even snuck pictures from the family album as proof because I was determined to make the cruel middle school children understand that my life and upbringing were as rich as could be.

Although it was a big transition from the life we'd lived, I managed to overcome every mistreatment and every joke to prove to them that I was better than they thought. My feelings were hurt, but I never let them know how I felt. I would find whatever strength I could muster up to make it through the day and come home to cry under my covers. I was determined not to allow their words and meanness break me down. My focus was to learn to speak the language with a minimal accent. By day, I was in English Speaking Other Language classes (ESOL); by night, it was *The Brady Bunch* and *I Love Lucy*. In between, I read every book I could get my hands on. I didn't know I could borrow books from the library, during study hall and lunch, I would go to the school library and read as much as I could. At home, we received subscriptions for *Reader's Digest*. Some of the stories were a bit adult, but I still read them. For me, it wasn't about the content; it was about knowing how to read and speak English.

Adjusting to the Idea of a Stepmom

As much as I was excited to reunite with my dad, it was confusing and overwhelming because there was never a conversation about my mom or my stepmom. The painful part of this transition was that no one had spoken with my siblings and me about what was happening. And it didn't help that I was still stuck on the idea that very soon, my mom would join us. When it was time to board the plane, although my stepmom was with us, my heart was waiting for the surprise that my mom would be coming. When we arrived in America with no sign of her, I suppressed my feelings and moved on with the plans set for us, as I always had done.

Upon our arrival, we stayed with my dad's best friend and his family for a few months while my dad found us a place to live. His best friend was Ethiopian, and it was easy to find comfort with him; but his wife was American, and I felt she had agreed to more than she had bargained for. Suddenly, to have two adults and four children in her home for an unknown amount of time was a lot. As if the move wasn't traumatizing enough, staying with another family made things even more awkward. For a few months, we walked on pins and needles. We felt uncomfortable running water, turning on lights, or watching TV. Although we were hungry, we could not freely go to the kitchen and prepare something to eat. It didn't help that when we talked, she felt uncomfortable, especially when we spoke with her husband in our native language.

Because my transcripts were missing, I couldn't start school on schedule, so I was home a little longer, and it always felt like we were in her way. To make matters worse for me, staying home with my stepmother, we silently battled one another, because in my heart, I blamed her for my mom not coming with us. She was nice, but she was someone I didn't know. The only thing I knew about her was that she got in the way of my mom's opportunity to reunite with my dad.

For years, we quietly conflicted with one another over small things. Just as my siblings and I had a hard time adjusting to her, she also had a difficult time adapting to her new life. I can't imagine her fears of entering a new marriage with four children who lived a traumatized childhood due to their parents' separation and many hurts in life. To top that off, she became pregnant during our first year in America, and soon we had a new baby added to the transition. But he was a blessing God used to bring healing to our home. A year or so after my baby brother was born, my stepmom started a new job, making me his caregiver at the age of 15. During the season when my siblings and I were separated from our parents, I had taken on the motherly role emotionally, so that experience naturally came into play with my new little brother. In the absence of my stepmom, I was responsible for taking him to the babysitter, doctor's visits, and the playground, as well as bathing him and getting him ready for bed. My baby brother and I became inseparable. He didn't eat unless I fed him; he didn't sleep unless I rocked him. When he was out with his mom, he made sure I received flowers, even though he picked dandelions. In some ways, he became like my child when I was 15.

With a little strain in our relationship, my stepmother and I began to make the best of what we had, but occasionally, there was friction because boundaries and expectations were not made clear in the home. As I mentioned, as children, we didn't have a voice. You submitted to the plans and ideas your parents put in place, so I did not have clarity. My struggle had been the fact that after all those years, I did not want to give my dad up again, this time to a strange woman. Eventually, my dad had to put his foot down and remind us that she was his wife, and that we were his children. He said, "Listen, when I'm older and something happens to me, you're going to be off on your own, and she is going to be the one taking care of me. Whether you like it or not, you're going to have to respect her." I appreciated him saying that because it is exactly what happened. Throughout my dad's sickness, my stepmom was there through thick and thin. She took care of him with kindness until the day he took his last breath. And by God's divine intervention, my relationship with her ultimately improved after my baby brother was born. Our relationship grew even closer as I realized how kind she was to my dad and how much she cared about my siblings and me despite our reactions toward her.

Honoring Your Given Name

Soon, I began school and met my friend Retana, who'd immigrated from Thailand and understood what it meant to assimilate into a new culture. She took me under her wings and defended me. She also said my name was too difficult to pronounce and wanted to give me a nickname. She said I reminded her of Lisa-Lisa of the Cult Jam, a musical group from the 1980s; therefore, she would begin calling me Lisa. I wasn't going to change my name, but since she was my best friend, I allowed her to give me a nickname. "Only between you and me," I said. I didn't know she had told the whole school my name was Lisa, so when I heard Lisa, I didn't answer because I wasn't expecting to be called anything other than my given name. I was bullied and called conceited for not answering to Lisa, and eventually, I grew tired of it. To fit in with my new culture and teen life, I accepted the nickname and became Lisa in the hallways and on the playground. Although I never officially changed my name, I was known to my classmates and teachers as Lisa. Afraid that my dad would be upset with me, I did not tell him why I was using a different name. During graduation, I requested for my name to be listed as Lisa (Hirut). It was important for me to maintain my given name but still be part of the community I was in.

The nickname stayed with me until my 30th birthday, after which I began to understand the beauty of my roots, family culture, and origin. Since the day I'd agreed to accept Lisa as my nickname, I found myself explaining and justifying why I was not using my given name. In Ethiopian culture, your name is associated with your destiny and purpose, but I just wanted to fit in. My focus had been to become Americanized, but I realized I was denying who I was and shunning the beauty of my rich culture and heritage. As I became accustomed to my new world, I began to find that peace and acceptance I had often desired. I was motivated to reach greater heights in my journey into adolescence and to walk in the newness of life that God had appointed for me. I am proud of the name my parents gave me: Hirut—a derivative of Ruth in the book of the Bible, meaning friendship.

REFLECTIONS

For me, it was important early on to learn how to take life's transitions with grace. Transitions are impossible to avoid. They follow you through life, and how you respond to each moment determines your strength and where you will land while dealing with all obstacles—including abandonment and rejection. You see, all the choices we make have the potential to affect our lives and those around us for years to come.

THOUGHTS FOR YOUR JOURNEY

Everyday life seems to bring in a new transition. How do you take each moment and make it valuable to who you are? Who are you, and where is the pride that you have been assigned to carry?

"Remember not the former things, nor consider the things of old. Behold, I am doing a new thing; now it springs forth, do you not perceive it? I will make a way in the wilderness and rivers in the desert."

Isaiah 43:18–19

"A good name is to be chosen rather than great riches, loving favor rather than silver and gold."

Proverbs 22:1

Riding through life as a team

Standing tall and glowing in God's love

CHAPTER 5

SOARING THROUGH THE SEASONS

Progressing Through Life's Adventures

After my transition to a new country, having to adjust to a new home life and surviving middle school as a new immigrant, life was moving to a new season, as expected. I became more comfortable with the culture and, of course, my goal was to fit in as a teenager in all aspects of high school. I began to understand the difference in how people responded to the name Lisa; therefore, I continued using my nickname, and I made the effort to participate in all school-wide activities. High school was a different type of monster, but I managed to balance everything, kept my eyes on my future success, and took steps forward. While learning during the day and working a part-time job at Wendy's fast-food restaurant, I felt like I was excelling; having my own money as a teenager was empowering. My first role at Wendy's was as a dining room hostess. A few months later, I was moved to the frontline runner and eventually promoted to cashier. Dad was my example of a great work ethic. Through him, I learned how to excel at the opportunities presented to me.

My commitment to my job pleased my manager, and as I recommended my sister and best friends, they were hired literally on the spot. Today, each one of us are in a place of success and satisfied with our professional journey. During my senior year, I transitioned to Bradlees department store and later to Montgomery Ward. With each employment, my roles and responsibilities significantly changed. Suddenly, I started to develop the attitude of a typical teenager. My style of clothing changed; make-up and jewelry became part of my daily routine. However, as I watched my classmates prepare to leave home for college to experience their independence, I began to feel empty. I constantly wondered how I could find a way to go to college because being left behind wasn't a good feeling. As an uneducated parent, Dad didn't know the options that were available to me.

While my friends completed college applications and financial aid forms and visited campuses, I continued to work to save for senior year activities because that was my only attainable goal at that time. However, as I began to mature through each experience of life, I started to research my options to encounter the journey of my college-bound friends. Financially, my only attainable plan was to enroll in a one-year program at Yorktown Business Institute to pursue a certificate in office automation. After graduating from my one-year program, I found my first professional job at a Fortune 500 IT company in a temporary-to-permanent position as an office assistant, which marked the beginning of my new professional journey. A year later, I landed a full-time job at a nonprofit Greek organization in Washington, D.C., as an administrative assistant to the executive director of the membership department. The experience I gained from each job expanded my interest in an HR role. Two years later, I transitioned to one of the largest accounting firms in the Washington, D.C., area, in a position that lasted for six years. Then, as a result of a company reorganization, I was back to square one again, hunting for a job. Thank God, I was quickly able to find an HR Administrative Assistant position at the IT company that had given me my first professional experience as a temp.

I eventually grew into various HR roles, working directly under the human resources vice president and employee awards programs sponsored by the division president. Of course, a four-year college degree was always at the forefront of my mind, and I was determined that one day, I would graduate with that degree. While working full-time, I enrolled at Prince George's Community College to begin my education. While in my roles as a wife, a mom to a preteen and a toddler, and a leader at my church, 10 years later, I persevered and received my AA degree in business management and began preparation for my long-term goal of acquiring a BS, which I ultimately completed and received my four-year degree in business management.

Understanding the Dynamics of My Body

The experience of puberty is a season of life I faced without any preparation or guidance. Such a unique and important stage in the life of a young lady that requires the support of a mother or a mother figure. It was the weirdest time of my life, filled with so many emotions that went up and down unexpectedly.

Imagine growing up with severe pain every month, an ordeal that became part of my journey when I was nine years old, and no one knew what was happening to me. During this season of life, the presence of my mother was so desired but was nowhere to be found. I had so many questions but never knew who or what to ask. I was an emotional wreck. Depression and anxiety started rooting in me. In addition to the emotional challenges, the physical pain became severe and unbearable. I often tucked my head between my knees each month, trying to brace myself for the pain. Little did I know, I was experiencing a young lady's normal growth process into adolescence; but what made my situation difficult was that no one knew I was developing endometriosis, which was formally diagnosed in me at the age of 17. Thank God for my school nurse, who took the time to listen and provide safe guidance. After bringing a note to my father suggesting that I be examined, I was taken to George Washington Hospital, where I received my diagnosis and started my journey with medical treatments, which included a series of surgeries.

During this time of growth, I needed my mom to embrace me and to share the things my mind and body were experiencing, to teach me about womanhood and other things in life that a young lady must know. But the absence of my mom had such an impact on my life and eventually on my self-esteem.

My school nurse was my lifesaver and sounding board. Upon her recommendation, I went to the doctor. After each appointment, I would give the nurse my update, and she, in turn, would give me questions to ask. It was a trying season of life. I began to wonder what was wrong with me, but I continued to hope that it would eventually heal and that I could be normal like everyone else.

After years of doctor visits, I received the first piece of the devastating news that disturbed my youthful dreams. As my doctor visits became more frequent, fear was becoming evident. I remember moments of loneliness while sitting in examination rooms and wearing a thin paper gown. My mind traveled through every fearful possibility as I looked up at the medical pictures hanging on the walls, overwhelmed with the fear of a negative report. As a young girl with no mother to hold my hand, I cried and wished I was not alone. In icy-cold rooms, with the ache of my little tender heart, I was forced to become an adult, and at the end of several appointments and several surgeries, doctors declared everything should be fine. However, I was also introduced to the small possibility of infertility problems later in life.

Correcting the current physical issue with surgeries to minimize the monthly cramping was promising. However, not having someone to advocate on my behalf was such a disadvantage. I'll never forget a student doctor telling me that when I became sexually active, my body would adjust. My young mind was in a state of confusion. Fear of the unknown was paralyzing. Imagine carrying such a load at the age of 17. Holding my tears and clutching my broken heart, I scheduled my next appointment and took the D4 bus home, pretending everything was normal. As I observed every woman and wondered if they knew what was going on in my world, I was so overwhelmed and embarrassed I did not know whom to trust with this scary news. Night after night, I cried and went to sleep with the fear of what my future would be. My dad sensed that things were becoming more than I could handle and asked his best friend's wife to go with me to my next appointment. I was relieved because everything had become so cloudy; I needed someone there.

The pain and disappointment of not having a bond with the mother who birthed me and nursed me have been a sensitive reality all my life, even as an adult. Every day, I woke up wondering what it would have been like to be raised by her. Missing the opportunity of sharing my future and the possibility of facing difficulties with motherhood was a struggle. Having to tell my father the outcome of my medical visits and explain the next steps in my painful journey was a sad reminder that I needed my mom. I felt the beginning of my womanhood being challenged, and although I hadn't done anything wrong, I felt like it was my fault. However, for the sake of surviving, I learned to tolerate the unknown.

I wrapped my fears in faith and moved forward with the life God gave me. In 1985, I had major surgery to correct my issues. For the first time, I felt like a normal teenage girl, and the extreme pain subsided significantly. As much as I wanted to believe in a miracle, fear of the unknown was overwhelming, and it marked the beginning of my painful infertility journey. The heart that had once believed in miracles became discouraged, but still, a small possibility of God changing the odds gave me comfort.

The Power of Friendships

Authentic friendships have always been priceless and immeasurable to me because you cannot put a value on them, and they have no boundaries. God-ordained friendships will keep giving through good and bad times; they will always find a way to thrive. My experience of friendships has been a journey of development, maturity, and change. With each one, my perspective and understanding of myself and others have been expanded and renewed. I have learned more about my ability to love as the Lord desires me to love, and my purpose in life has been magnified and fulfilled.

Friendships change depending on the individual's journey, and with each change, you gain or lose a friend.

I learned not to take any of it personally because people change—including myself. However, true friendship is maintained without any hardship, and if friends must be apart for a season or indefinitely, the friendship is sustained healthily and respectfully.

For me, authentic friendships are the heart of who I am. By nature, God has created me with the will and ability to love, nurture, and serve others, regardless of their background. *Thriving friendships are a two-way ministry; as you give, you must also receive.* I give God praise for calling me into such a role. I learned early in life to be my own friend and love who I am despite any shortcomings in my own life. Learning to accept, love, and value who I am has allowed me to accept, love, and value others. I have many friends in a variety of seasons and ages, and amazingly, God has blessed me to be able to meet each friend right where she is and to love without comparison. I can specifically point out the value of each person who has crossed my path. Some have been a pillar, no matter what; they stand strong and weather through the seasons. Others are like seasonal flowers that sit silently and make an appearance when life happens and when they are needed the most. I find both of those groups to be necessary for the person that I have become.

Discovering Love

It is part of normal development for a girl to have crushes in life. Since birth, my first love was always my dad. However, my first crush was around the age of 12, when I was fascinated by a young man who lived in our neighborhood and attended the same school. He lived on the other side of our street and had to pass by our house to get to school. Every morning, I would intentionally be late so I could walk with him. To tell you the truth, I am not sure if he ever saw me or recognized I was there. Most of my life has been making the effort to be seen and heard, but the one thing that I was missing in life was that God sees me for who He created me to be.

High school was a defining moment for me, a season of life when I decided to give love a try. Although it was culturally taboo, in secret, I took a chance and had a high school sweetheart. The first time I thought I was in love and acted on it was during my 10th-grade year. Not understanding the impact of the emotional stress and heartbreak that could come with such an emotional entanglement at a young age and not foreseeing the consequences, I placed myself in a vulnerable position. Unknowingly, I stepped into adult territory that was beyond my comprehension. By the end of my junior year, what I had feared happened. My young love life shifted to heartbreak and disappointment. I was hurt. I remember telling my best friends, "I am done!" At that point, I made myself a promise not to have a crush on any guy again. You see, my first experience of separation and breakup was with my mom and dad, and although I outgrew my childhood, the emotional pain secretly traveled with me throughout my life.

REFLECTIONS

Eventually, I outgrew the pain but never forgot the experience. Although I was traumatized at every level, God in his sovereignty has kept me. I was angry at the past and at others, but to experience God's pure blessings and forgiveness is my key to life's freedom. My primary goal in life became to choose my healing, embrace my circumstances, forgive those that have hurt me, and find what good could come from my struggles.

Seasons of life are a time of transition from one life event to another. Every experience gained in each season is a catalyst for growth and self-discovery. Some seasons are more challenging than others; however, the path that we choose impacts our destination.

THOUGHTS FOR YOUR JOURNEY

I made a choice not to allow the seasons of life to overshadow my purpose in life. What can you do differently to soar through your seasons into victory?

"To everything there is a season. A time for every purpose under heaven."

Ecclesiastes 3:1

Smiling in the face of adversity

My hearts, my family!

Dance with my favorite guys at my 25th wedding anniversary celebration--
my baby brother and the youngest grandchild represent my late dad

My long-awaited goal accomplishment, graduating with my BS in Business Management in 2021

CHAPTER 6
THE MEANING OF TRUE LOVE

My marriage story began when I was little. I always dreamed of having a big family and a home with a mom and a dad. I decided in my heart that my kids would never have to answer questions about whether their dad existed and whether they were loved. As I got older, that dream never died. Each time I had a crush on a boy, I imagined them as my husband, and I dreamed of the type of wife and mother I would become. All my childhood playtime activities involved playing house.

A Lasting Love: My Forever and Always

Tony and I met during a blind date in 1984 at Landover Mall. Although I had heard that he was a great guy, I had zero attraction toward him. I had certain expectations, but Tony didn't fit any of the things that I had on my list. I had reservations and pursued other relationships, but in the end, Tony always turned out to be the best choice for me. *He pursued me with passion and confidence*. Slowly, he began to grow on me, and I started to let my guard down and re-evaluated my expectations against reality. Meeting his mom gave me some clarity and direction with my decision about him. His mom always made me feel special and still does now. Tony was very attentive to me and made sure that his pursuit of me was clear. As time went on, he and I became close friends and made the decision to be exclusive. While he was away during his boot camp training in the United States Marines, we continued to nurture our friendship by writing sweet love letters back and forth. My very first out-of-town trip since I had moved to the United States was to his boot camp graduation in Parris Island, South Carolina. Although by now I was convinced he had some good qualities that I would love to have in a friend and possibly in a future husband, there was still a bit of doubt in me, and I wondered if I was making the right decision. Therefore, I took it slowly, but I never let go of him.

At that time, Tony sang in a community choir, and I often attended their meetings to support him. After every choir event, we discussed what had taken place in the service, and our conversation always ended with us talking about salvation. We began having Bible studies, and one Tuesday night after our one-on-one Bible study, Tony shared the gospel with me, and I invited Christ to come into my life since that moment, things have never been the same. I eventually joined the choir.

Because we chose to make God the foundation of our friendship, we were respectful toward one another and often evaluated our boundaries. We made time to talk every day about everything in life. We intentionally made time to plan outings. We took road trips, sometimes with no destination in mind. There were days we drove until we were tired, took a nap at a rest stop, and turned around. During our rides, we talked about where we had been and where we would like to be. Then, eight years into our friendship, he casually proposed after one of our late-night phone chats. I said, "Yes," and in 1991, at the age of 25, I married my best friend and the future father of the "many" children I imagined having. Happy as I could be, I walked into my fairy-tale life while carrying a small piece of doubt and fear in my mind about the possibility of infertility. I smiled, hoped, and believed God would work it out, and I skipped happily into ever after as Mrs. Thompson with the confidence and authority that *we got this!*

Our wedding was the most beautiful and spiritual event I had ever seen. It was a blessed experience and a testimony to what God can do. Following our wedding ceremony, we observed the Ethiopian tradition and planned another celebration called "Melse", which is for immediate family and close friends to get to know the newlyweds and their extended families.

I remember a family member saying, "You accomplished so much in your youthful age. What more can you ask for?" I smiled and said, "CHILDREN." At the same moment, I was replaying the doctor's discouraging words on the possibility of infertility. I was determined not to allow the words of a mere man to get the core of what I believed and hoped. I continued pressing toward the plan I knew God had for me.

The Beginning of Happily Ever After

Year one was a blast. We were having so much fun trying to figure out life together. We were fascinated with the idea of serving one another, sharing a meal daily, going to church holding hands, and learning one another's shortcomings and love points. Many of our dates were conversations about our upbringing, fears, disappointments, and hopes for our future. No matter what curveballs life brought our way, we promised we'd always remember we are married to God first. We made a conscious decision to make sure that God was the main point. During courting, our dates involved fasting and praying, going to an open park to have Bible study, and finding spiritual activities that promoted our development while we enjoyed each other's presence. *We had no fears or insecurities because our commitment was and is for God and with God*. Although we are opposites—I am a social butterfly and like to be where the happenings are, and he is calm and enjoys smaller crowds and quiet places— to please one another, we learned to adapt to each other's ways and wishes. The key to our relationship is that we are friends first. We fight together, love together, and serve together. We are proof you can have a good marriage and family even if you've experienced unsuccessful examples of marriage. You don't have to repeat history because you have learned from it.

The more Tony exposed me to God and His word, the more I saw our lives changing before my eyes. We made a commitment to go to church together. After we were married in September of 1991, the Lord led us to New Song Bible Fellowship Church in March 1992, where we received the right hand of fellowship. The best decision we made was to find this neutral place of worship, which allowed us to start fresh. Church became and continues to be the foundation for our marriage. It allows us to grow with one another through our ups and downs in the most beautiful way.

REFLECTIONS

True love is a strong and lasting bond between a couple in a passionate relationship. It allows you to express love without any expectations or limits. It gives you the power to respect and honor each other's boundaries and roles. It will also motivate you to care for and nurture the others above your own self.

THOUGHTS FOR YOUR JOURNEY

How do you view your love relationship, and what goals and boundaries have you set to grow with your marriage and protect it from all obstacles?

"Love suffers long and is kind; love does not envy; love does not parade itself, is not puffed up; does not behave rudely, does not seek its own, is not provoked, thinks no evil."
1 Corinthians 13:4–5

Cutting our fabulous wedding cake   *Just arrived at my wedding reception*

Family on the wedding day

Photo taken after Tony's Bootcamp graduation

CHAPTER 7

THE BLESSING OF CHILDREN

Throughout the Bible, God is clear that children are a gift that He has given to the family. God uses children to teach us how to show His love, grace, mercy, and forgiveness. Whether you are a biological, adopted, or foster parent, God has specially chosen you to be the recipient of this special gift He created for you to nurture and fulfill His purpose for this world. *Children matter, and they are a treasure that will keep on giving*.

The Calling to Parenthood

As newlyweds, we were not against having children right away. Our hopes and prayers were that the medical concerns would be resolved within the first year of our marriage, and that we would be ready to start our family. While waiting, we chose to focus on each other and build our bond for what may be ahead. Being members of a small and young church, we had high expectations because of the seasons most of our members were in. When my husband and I joined this sweet church six months after we said,

"I do," there was an expectation and pressure for us to start a family. We were often asked, "Where is the baby?" and "What are you waiting for?" I tried to make light of the situation, but on the inside, I was struggling because each time I was asked, it validated the idea that there may be some issues. I love kids, and my vision has always been to have a large family. I faithfully kept a calendar and a prayer journal. I followed the advice of my doctors while I battled in my mind daily. It was hard to understand what was happening with my body. I often felt like I owed others a justification as to why things weren't successful.

Throughout my 20s and 30s, I began to own the fact that there *could* be a problem, and the idea we may not have children was becoming real. As I turned the pages of my mind to the experience of my teenage years and the struggle with endometriosis, it was evident, and I was certain the issue was beyond my understanding. I feared that my marriage may take a turn in the wrong direction, and I began to blame myself. The process of medical appointments, tests, procedures, reading and researching information to find out the possible problem, and maintaining hope for a resolution was traumatic. Eventually, we decided to pursue infertility treatments, which were more than a notion. I remember sitting in doctors' offices with half the waiting room full of pregnant women and wondering, *Why not me?* I had so many questions but no tangible answers.

Through this journey, my husband was the best gift that God had given me. ***Without complaining, murmuring, and***

72

despising me, he walked through the process with compassion and care. He did not shun me; instead, he taught me how to walk with faith and push through to victory. With the utmost respect and honor, my husband showed me love and elevated me. I felt valued and loved by him, regardless of the medical challenges that we were possibly facing. His love has always been brand new through every season of our journey. Repeatedly, he assured me that everything would work out. He said we were a team, and in this game of life, if God chose not to allow us to parent biologically, He would provide the choice of His heart and fill our arms and homes with love.

His willingness to surrender to God's will gave me the ability and the desire to yield to the idea of adoption. Was it a simple decision? Certainly not! Although adoption is an awesome idea, since childhood, it had been my dream to have my own children. I had a grand idea of how I would announce my pregnancy to my husband and to the world, the type of baby shower I would have, and how I would make my entrance. I'd picked out Ethiopian names: For a girl, Tigist (meaning patience) Joy Thompson because I waited for her patiently, and for a boy, Tamirat (meaning miracle) Hope Thompson because my life is full of miracles. But the reality of being childless was becoming too real. It was scary to process and difficult to accept, but every step of the journey was orchestrated by the grace and love of God.

When Life Doesn't Make Sense

Ten years after my first surgery, I developed fibroids and scar tissue, leading me to go under the knife a second time in 1998. The only difference this time was I had a support system in my sweetest best friend and sister, the late Pam Dodson. With her by my side, every appointment felt easy and safe. I can still see it like it was yesterday. She spoke life into me, driving up and down to and from Georgetown Hospital. I never had to experience the lonely feeling I had in examination rooms. When I was overwhelmed and scared to ask questions, she was my mouthpiece. She was by my side for every procedure, there to wipe my tears, clean my wounds, listen to my complaints, and become the mother's shoulder I yearned for. She came home and explained every detail to my husband. The surgery was a major life-changing experience, as I was blessed to have her by my side. God's plan was becoming more and more evident in our journey. As smart as my doctors were, they couldn't explain what the issues were and what we had to do to get over them. Test after test, procedure after procedure revealed my body was fine. So once again, I was left with the question of "why". It was not to question God's authority, but desiring to understand His heart and plans for us.

During this season, just about every girlfriend and church member was having babies left and right. I knew that I was in the will of God when I found myself rejoicing for others with a heart of purity and genuine joy. For some, I was invited into the birthing room or the hospital; for others, I'd been asked to become a godparent. Each time, **God gathered my brokenness and used me to minister to others**. Those were the moments when God's love was beyond evident.

Throughout our journey, Tony and I reciprocated compassion and love for each other, and the process made us love one another even more. As we considered whether to continue and undergo infertility treatments, we were hesitant. We did everything except the very last step when we both, in agreement, felt uncomfortable in our spirits. For us, it was more important to be in the perfect will of God rather than a permissive will; therefore, we made an agreement to adopt.

God's Voice and His Choice for My Life

Understanding the voice of God through my journey of infertility, *I learned to live in peace despite my "whys."* I am convinced and delighted that my journey is not wasted. I had the honor of using my pain to bring pleasure to God and minister to others who are struggling with unexpected life challenges. Accepting and working through the cards life dealt me were the keys to my breakthrough, but I always had faith that a miracle would take place. *And in so many ways, it did.* God has given me such pride in the journey He called me into. Even though the unknown was a huge concern, it never kept me up. I learned at an early age to walk in my truth and calling and to see every circumstance as a path to greatness.

My goal in life remained that no matter what, I would not let circumstances defeat me. I thought if God had given me the desire to be a mother and made me a nurturer, He must have other plans, and with that thought, while we still hoped and prayed for God to bless us with children the natural way, we decided to move forward with adoption. Just then, my younger brother had a daughter he asked us to help with. Suddenly, our focus changed. We had no time to worry about anything else—we had a child to care for.

You Can't Beat God's Giving Double Blessings

We started keeping our oldest niece on weekends and holidays when she was two years old. Eventually, when she was six years old, we began the process of making her ours. I am super grateful that her parents chose her well-being and gave us formal guardianship, which made the process manageable. When she was 10 years old, we were able to finalize her adoption, and she became our daughter legally.

Despite not being our biological child, I am amazed at how much she reminded me of myself at that age. Although she loved to be with us, she was still longing for her parents. Like her, I didn't care where my parents were in life; I wanted to be with them. I knew the emptiness she felt not having that emotional connection with her parents. Although we did everything we could for her, she always yearned for her parents and wondered when they would come for her. We had an open dialogue with her about why she was with us, and we did the best we could to keep her engaged with her extended family. But after a while, we had to rethink that idea because it started to impact her negatively. As her guardians, we continued supporting her in every way until she settled, not just physically, but emotionally as well.

Though it was a blessing for her to be with us, she had a hard time with the adoption. In her mind, that meant she was forever separated from her biological parents. Although you learn to manage them, the unfortunate part of these types of experiences are that they always find a way to resurface. You can't separate yourself from the internal heartache. As much as she loved being with us, her heart and emotions always bled for her biological parents. She was loyal to them, but at the same time, she respected and honored us.

While we were getting our older daughter established, we were blessed with her little sister. The day I met her, she walked into our house and claimed our hearts and home. From that moment on, she instantly became the fourth member of our sweet household. She loved the idea of becoming part of a stable household. While we began our preparation to adjust our everyday routine to be available to raise a 19-month-old baby who was still in diapers, she snuck up into our hearts, and we all fell in love with her just as much as she had with us. Although she had her own room, in the mornings, we often found her tucked in with her sister.

In the meantime, we immediately began our search for daycare and started the legal process for her adoption. Having experienced the headaches and heartache of guardianship, we decided to obtain legal counsel to assist us with the process. The system wasn't any better, but this time, we had someone on our side who fully understood the law and knew how to lead us through the hurdles. By the grace and favor of God, we were able to complete the process of guardianship in time to enroll her in a pre-k program.

She loved the idea of waking up in the morning and dressing up with whatever she could get her hands on—as long as it had her favorite colors, she was okay with it. She'd pull her hair back with a tie, put a juice box and a bag of skittles in her lunch bag for the day's journey, and say, "I'm ready, Mom!" Our oldest was very reserved and calculated in how she gave and received love. However, the youngest was an open book, very vocal and generous in dispensing affection. For her, it was important to immediately identify us as her mom and dad, while for the oldest, we were Auntie and Uncle for the longest time. Even though she finally adjusted to becoming our daughter, emotionally, it was and still is a struggle for her to overcome her status.

For both our daughters, regardless of their personalities and background, belonging to a family was a dream come true, just as it was for Tony and me. They brought such joy and balance to our home, and God used them to fulfill our desire to parent. Even as an adult, I recall wishing and hoping I belonged to someone. I secretly adopted my friends' moms because it gave me a sense of belonging and identity with someone who was important to me. Although we didn't understand God's plan and process at first, we are so elated that He chose us to partner with Him to fulfill His desire for our daughters. With our two princesses, our lives and home have never been the same.

Although my heart still cried out to God for an understanding of His plans and vision for my life in the area of mothering, He chose my husband and me to parent in a very special way—from His heart to our arms. *It's awesome when you know that you are called out for the ordinary, but it's different when you are called out for the extraordinary.* This is when you know that your life is a calling. My own grief from not being able to have my own mom is always something that I must deal with. However, through my own journey, I learned that being a mother is more than I knew.

For a long time, I struggled with the "whys." The month of May was always a roller coaster of emotions for me. I made every effort to avoid the greeting card aisle on Mother's Day. As I would shop for gifts or cards for mother figures in my life, I often choked up with tears and had meltdowns when I returned home. My most embarrassing moments occurred at church when moms were asked to stand up during acknowledgments and gift-giving. While I was happy for others, I felt like I didn't deserve the recognition even though I was a mother of two beautiful daughters. It became so painful, but I always managed to put on the most genuine and biggest smile that I could muster up while I wrestled with God in my heart to make it through the longest two hours.

Eventually, I stopped going to church on Mother's Day. Instead, my husband would find ways to make my day lighthearted and save my emotions. He and the girls pampered me with spa outings, showered me with Mother's Day gifts, and made me feel like I was the only person that was being celebrated that day. After some time, by God's intervention and due to the sensitivity of my Pastor, suddenly, Mother's Day was celebrated differently at church—highlighting all mothers and mother figures, which is well deserved. It might be something small, but for me, it was huge!

Reading the cry of Hannah in the Book of 1 Samuel, it was obvious that God loved her. As she cried out to him from the depth of her soul, He answered her prayers, not when and how she wanted, but nonetheless, He answered her according to His plan. Hannah was also loved tremendously by her husband. Regardless of her challenges, he loved her, and he was fully committed to her. In the same way, my husband never belittled me or made me feel like less than a woman. He always elevated me and was never embarrassed by the choices God made for us. Through our struggles, our connection only grew stronger. We owned our calling as a team, and God honored us every step of the way. We accepted God's choice as the best choice for us.

I am thankful that God chose me to be my husband's wife and that my children came to me as they did. Without a doubt in our hearts, His choice for us was to raise the children of His heart. Our journey was never a secret to our children. It's important to us that they are aware of how important they are and what lengths God took to provide for them. Because we allowed God to have His way, we walk in completeness and with pleasure. We raised the children of His choice for us. He had us in mind when He created them. To be honest, sometimes we even forget that we didn't birth them.

I remember asking the Lord once, "Why am I in this place? Why could I not have had just one child?" God's answer was clear. He reminded me that if I had even one child, I would be so consumed with my own that they will not be a priority. God knew the emotion and heart space needed for my daughters. I remember being in awe, and that day, I had to ask God for forgiveness. They are a gift that came without any regrets or hardship.

REFLECTIONS

As married young adults, we had a dream of having several children, and we set goals and made plans on the type of family we would be. Unfortunately, we didn't make room for God's plan. Through our daughters, God erased years of my heartache and trauma. With God's grace, we made it; we put them through school and had the joy of experiencing the role of parenting God's way. We had all the beautiful traditions we'd dreamed of having as a family in the eyes of God. It may not have come to us exactly in the way I'd imagined, but the beauty of life came to us even more perfectly as God intended.

THOUGHTS FOR YOUR JOURNEY

Ready or not, the reality of life comes. You and I will never know what is ahead until we reach that point. My take on life is to always trust God's heart and the plans He has identified for me and expect God to shine through me so others can be blessed. When have you courageously persevered despite never experiencing something that you longed for? Somebody needs to know how you got over it.

"A man's heart plans his way, But the Lord directs his steps."

Proverbs 16:9

"He grants the barren woman a home, Like a joyful mother of children."

Psalm 113:9

My Babies, My saving Grace and Loves

My hubby and daughters after we visited The White House during Barak Obama's presidency

My heart beats, my jewels, my blessings, my daughters

Tony and I celebrating our 25th wedding anniversary vow renewal and our 50th birthday with our beautiful families

CHAPTER 8

PARENTING OUR PARENTS

Throughout our marriage, while raising our daughters, we had the honor and joy of caring for our aging parents.

The Experience of Dad-and-Daughter World

In the early 1990s, my father's health began to fail, and his doctor's visits became more frequent. Although he had lived in America for more than 40 years, he held tightly to his culture and had so much pride that he did not allow my stepmom or us, as his children, to become involved in his care. After receiving several calls from his doctors and seeing his health decline, my stepmom suggested that I get involved, and she would support my decisions.

All my life, I'd looked for my dad to be my parent, and when I found him, I became his. It is interesting how quickly roles in life change. It was the most humbling and vulnerable experience of both our lives, especially for my dad. Coming from a culture where gender roles were clearly defined, where men assumed the most authority and women were subordinate, just imagine my dad's struggle to yield his independence to his wife and daughter. In general, parents and elders are highly respected and honored in Ethiopia, so for me to have to assist my dad physically at his lowest point was difficult because a daughter shouldn't see her dad in that light. However, love trumps all cultural and personal standards, and today, I look back and praise God for the opportunity, in the absence of my older brother, to be used to love and serve my dad beyond my own abilities.

Dad is truly the most amazing and resilient person I have ever known. His life is a testimony to God's grace and love. Even with a third-grade education, he managed to beat all odds and live a successful life. Dad's radiant spirit and compassion for others endeared him to many. Growing up, he was known in his community as a true humanitarian who enjoyed helping others. His passion for people afforded him the opportunity to serve in whatever capacity he could. It has been an honor for me to care for my dad; his story is one to be told. He lived through many situations that were unbelievable.

In the early 1980s, Dad found himself in the middle of a gunpoint carjacking. He refused to give in and took off driving. Unfortunately, as he drove, the gun had already been released. Out of shock, Dad drove home from D.C., 30 minutes away, and climbed to the third floor of our apartment. I heard him fumble to open the door. I let him in, and he stumbled over to the couch and fell off.

Not knowing what was going on, my stepmom turned him over to find that his stomach was blown up to the top of his neck. We immediately called 911, and he was taken to Prince George's Trauma Center. Following several surgeries to remove the bullet and weeks of hospitalization, miraculously as always, Dad made it through.

Several years later, he was diagnosed with type 2 diabetes and prostate cancer, but after major surgeries and chemo treatment, he beat cancer. However, due to a lack of proper self-care and management, Dad's body eventually stopped producing insulin, causing him to depend on daily injections. Unfortunately, because of his diabetes, Dad battled other health issues, such as neuropathy, kidney failure, cataracts, amputation of his right leg, and so much more. My role as his caregiver quickly reached a necessary point. Between cleaning his diabetic wounds, three days of dialysis treatments, ongoing doctors' appointments, countless visits to emergency rooms, and many lonely moments in hospital waiting rooms hoping it was the last time, the struggles of trying to convince him to take his meds, eat food, and basically stay encouraged was stressful and scary.

Although aging is a blessing, it is more than losing physical abilities. Dad's struggle was about losing his independence in life. Having been the caregiver of himself and others since he could remember, suddenly being told he needed someone to care for him was beyond humbling. Aging is unavoidable, but who wants to hear that they are not capable of doing normal things in their 40s and 50s? In some ways, caring for Dad was made easier because my stepmom and I were a great team. She cared for him during the day, and Tony and I, as well as my baby brother, took over at night. I loved my dad, but he was the most difficult patient ever, and after so many incidents, we had to rethink our plans to properly care for him.

Making Hard Life Decisions

The pivotal moments that drove us to decide to admit Dad into a nursing home involved our inability to provide him with the constant medical attention he needed. Because we all worked full-time, it became difficult for us to monitor his day-to-day health episodes. Although his body was deteriorating, Dad's mind was still fully active, to the point that he thought he could still function normally and found himself in dangerous situations. He experienced life-threatening falls, blacked out while driving, and nearly went into a diabetic coma, just to mention a few incidents. As a result of the impact and the frequency of his diabetic episodes, we had to make a difficult decision to admit him into a nursing home, something that was looked down upon in our culture. But for his safety and for our sanity, we had no other options.

During the four years he was there, we did our best to make it comfortable for him. As a family, we made sure that we were present during our daily visits. We brought him his favorite foods, washed his clothes, and made some surprise pop-ups to show our presence. During holidays, we picked him up or spent the day with him at the facility. While he was there, he had several procedures, including a major surgery to amputate one of his legs up to the kneecap. But even with all that, Dad remained humorous and full of praises and gratitude to God for his life.

Dad was prepared to accept what God had in store for him. He was not afraid. He always had a positive outlook on life, and everything was wonderful in his eyes. When the time came for a family meeting to discuss last wishes, Dad said, "If Jesus comes for me, I don't want any of you to stand in the way. I have enjoyed my journey and lived a happy life." He didn't want to be resuscitated or have any type of intervention. Although Dad had a wish one day to move back home, he remained at the nursing and rehab facility until he took his last breath about four years after he was first admitted.

The Wind Beneath My Wing

December 7, 2014, is a day I can never erase from my mind. Years later, I can still see and hear the activities of that day. The Friday before the 7th, I'd taken Dad to a dialysis center for a procedure. At the end of his appointment, as he boarded the bus, he repeatedly said he loved me and began to pronounce blessings over me and my household. I was planning on following the driver back to the nursing home, but Dad suggested that I go back to work. I had a weird feeling, but I honored his wish. I told him I'd come to see him that following morning, but my stepmom decided to visit instead; so, I'd planned to go the next day. Around midnight, I received an unexpected phone call from the nursing home. When I called back, they said, "Disregard, Ms. Thompson. All is well. Your dad is resting." They reassured me that he was fine. However, as planned, my stepmom went to see him on Sunday morning, and she confirmed that he was doing well. After spending some time with him, he advised her to go home, and he went to his room.

That afternoon after church, I had a headache, and I was feeling strange. Five minutes after I laid down, I received another phone call from a staff member at Holy Cross Hospital. I jokingly asked if they knew I wasn't feeling well, but they said my dad had been brought in that afternoon. While my heart was skipping beats, I made my way to the hospital. Unfortunately, by the time I arrived, he was already gone. Fifteen minutes after he told my stepmom he was going to his room, my dad passed away from a pulmonary aneurysm.

He never allowed his physical limitations to stop him from enjoying life to its fullest. Even in his worst days, he was such a delight to be around, and I am so confident that he left this earth knowing he was loved and cared for. When he died, my life changed tremendously. The thought of never seeing him again on this side was incredibly sad, but I am comforted knowing that I will see him again one day. I loved and honored him and will always be Daddy's little girl.

The Ache for a Mother's Love

Rekindling my relationship with my dad meant the world to me, but the journey of finding my mom in my 30s whom I was separated from when I was seven years old was just as special. After locating Mom, I applied to bring her to the United States, and I was elated when she was approved. But unfortunately, during her embassy visit, they discovered she had breast cancer that had spread all over her body, and she was unable to travel. Hope turned into unbearable grief. Hearing the news, I crawled into bed in silent pain.

With the help of our family, friends, coworkers, and church, hubby and I were able to take a three-week trip to Ethiopia to learn more about her condition. When I first saw her, I wanted to cry with joy, but I had such a mix of emotions: happy, sad, angry, neglected, abandoned, hurt, and so much more.

It had been 23 years since I'd seen her, and she was sick to the point that she couldn't get in and out of bed. My mom was a stranger to me.

The next day, I saw her body while they cleaned her. The breast cancer had gotten so bad it had broken through her skin. It was more painful than I could handle, but to protect her, I managed to gather my emotions. I smiled while crying on the inside.

It felt like my mom was struggling to connect with me. I later found out that she felt uncomfortable hugging me and didn't want to touch me because she felt she was unclean. Hearing her say that made me love and respect her even more.

We decided to spend as much time as we could with her, and most days were spent sitting by her side talking. During my three weeks there, I gained a deeper understanding of and insight into my family history and dynamics, which helped me to make sense of many things in my life.

For years, I grew up assuming my mom didn't want me, but during that trip, I learned how much she yearned to find us. In fact, I learned that for 23 years, she had made it her purpose to search for us daily. Although she was forbidden to locate us due to our family politics, she never gave up hope.

As time passed, she was more and more fragile and in pain. I dressed her. We talked about each other's lives. We cried for the past and even for the future. My mom, as an only child, had loved children; and her plan was to have as many children as her health allowed and as she could.

Out of her 15 pregnancies, she lost one to miscarriage, one was stillborn, and lost the third baby to SIDS. Of the 12 of us, my younger brother died in a war fighting for his country, and one of our twin siblings died due to a life-threatening illness. Ten of us still live today. I remember sharing with Mom how I grew up motherless and had fears of being childless. But I also shared the plans that God had for us through our daughters and how thankful I am that the Lord, in His sovereignty, called us to the awesome role of raising them. All along, even in her own physical pain, I could see the ache in her heart for me as her oldest daughter.

I learned that she'd been sick for years, but she didn't think too much about it because her focus was on finding us. As the time for my return to the United States was approaching, the emotional struggle on both sides was evident. During our goodbyes, the sadness was overwhelming because I knew I was handing her over to death. We both were struggling with the separation; I could tell she was still feeling guilty. But in the end, God worked it out. She said goodbye without saying goodbye, which didn't hit me until after she had passed. When I got home, the Lord prompted me to send her a message of forgiveness, gratitude, and love to free her. I recorded a message to express how much I forgave, loved, and honored her and the joyful experience of the three weeks I'd had with her. I knew she didn't have much time on this earth, so it was important for me to share with her how much I was blessed to be with her.

Three weeks after my return, my husband and I had been out celebrating our anniversary. We were planning on having dinner, but something didn't feel right, so we decided to come home. In Ethiopian culture, you don't receive a call when someone dies. The elders of the community come to your door to make the announcement. My husband found out first and decided to break the news to me. Shortly after I heard, the family came over to comfort me. It was so unfair. I even questioned God, but His plans are His plans. It was such a huge hurt I thought I would never get over it, but time does heal all wounds. Each day, God gave me a different perspective on life, allowing me to move beyond the grief and honor her life for generations to come.

I sent money home to bury my mom, and as time went on, I accepted her passing, but I can never recover from the emptiness of losing her. I thank God for the opportunities I had to be able to sit at her feet and express my love and forgiveness. In those three weeks, God gave me everything I was missing for almost 30 years—the love, the gratification, and the story to share with the world. Now, I feel indebted to my family, to my half-brothers and sisters back home. We are linked together forever, and I'm sure we'll go back and visit again soon.

The Beauty of a Mother-in-Law (or Mother-in-Love)

Although my parents are gone, I am still blessed to be able to have a mother's love through my "mother-in-love," who has taken me under her wings and supported all my dreams and aspirations as though I am her daughter. She is truly a woman of honor and a walking testament to God's healing power. Although it was a major sacrifice for us to have her move in with us only five years after we said, "I do," it was a sacrifice that we do not regret. What a blessing it has been to have her be part of our journey. Let the truth be told, it was just as much of a sacrifice for her to be able to rely on her baby boy, especially as a newlywed.

During that season, her doctors felt her lupus was progressing and that she needed to go on medical disability. It was a life-changing experience for both of us, but throughout the process, love truly conquered all. It was not easy for her to give up her life of independence. And the experience wasn't easy for me either as I walked into the beginning of my new life as a woman and a wife. But we both understood that it was God's divine plan. While others were surprised when we decided to have her move in with us so early in our marriage, it has worked well for us. We are grateful she is still able to enjoy activities that make caring for her easier. She is an awesome mother and the best grandmother. The blessing of having her has gone beyond Tony and me, and it has blessed our children to experience a grandmother's love, prayers, and guidance. I enjoy her presence and prayers.

REFLECTIONS

A life cycle is real. Your parents raise you, and before you know it, you are on the giving rather than the receiving end. Although I wasn't raised by both my parents during the pinnacle part of life, the Lord made a way for me to experience the full cycle of what life offers because *I chose to walk into my future with forgiveness and freedom.* In the absence of my biological parents, God blessed me with a mother-in-love and other mentors to fill the gap that I was experiencing.

THOUGHTS FOR YOUR JOURNEY

I was intentional in loving and accepting my parents not for what they had done in life but because of who they were. And I remained open to God's provision to receive love from others. Who is it in your life that came short and didn't measure up to your standards but whom God desires for you to release so you can be free to receive your blessing?

"When my father and my mother forsake me, then the Lord will take care of me."

Psalm 27:10

My first visit home and first reunion with my mom after 22 years apart

Daddy and I on my wedding day, our happiest day together

My bonus moms, women of strength

CHAPTER 9

SHINE

God Never Fails

I am convinced that God's grace is truly sufficient in every situation, and His timing is always perfect. Even as an adult, when life gets tough, I rewind the tape of my mind to my childhood and remember how the power of God kept me.

Growing up without my parents was a trying season of life. With their divorce, my siblings and I lost stability, security, a place we once called home, trust in adults, and our own bonds with each other. Although the separation occurred when I was seven, I remember every detail of that season like it was yesterday. *Divorce is not something that happens only between husband and wife. Nor is it an experience of today that is forgotten tomorrow.* It is a painful journey that rips us apart from the inside out and creates lifelong trauma that disturbs emotional stability. Growing up, it made me question my value and purpose in life and created many other challenges; but by the grace of God, I made up my mind that I would learn from history and not repeat it.

For me, seeing life for what it is rather than what it could have been is a major blessing. Even though I didn't understand the Orthodox faith, I often went to church expecting answers from God, much like how I live my life now. Although God didn't have audible conversations with me, in my heart, I always felt a sense of relief and comfort knowing He heard me and would answer. God answers to every situation in life with a "yes", "no," or "not yet." Although my life's journey stayed mostly at "not yet," God never failed me, and His presence was more than evident. He answered my prayers differently than I expected, but it was much more rewarding than I could have imagined.

He reunited me with my parents in the most beautiful and tender way. He made my father's blessings in his last days of life illuminate the beauty of our relationship. He created an amazing and pure love experience between Tony and me. God has given me two beautiful and remarkable daughters as a gift from His heart. With each season of life, He has given me fulfillment in life; therefore, I choose to believe in God and praise Him through every situation.

Finding Life Through Grief

Losses and grief are typical parts of a person's life. Growing up, I lived through my share of losses, but each loss built a stronger me; it taught me to be resilient and courageous. Through each experience, my smile was my weapon. It was a sign of my strength overcoming the struggles I endured growing up. Every day, my goal in life became finding a reason to smile and walk in victory. Trusting in God beyond my natural understanding became important. God is real, and He can do anything but fail.

I was confident that joy would be part of my journey. I pressed through every obstacle that came my way as a person, a wife, a loving mom, and a faithful friend to everyone I encountered. I wanted to make sure other little girls did not feel alone, rejected, abandoned, or unnecessary. There are so many young ladies struggling through circumstances I've experienced. I want them to see the scars I wear physically and emotionally. I hold them high as my stamp of perseverance, but I never allow them to erase the strength and courage God has given me. I thank God for bringing the people He has brought on my journey—mentors who took me under their wings and poured into me.

No Weapon Formed Against Me

Although Satan tried to break me down, *God's love was and is always greater*. Even as an adult, despite Satan's attempts, God, in His sovereignty, changed the course of my path, even in life's most difficult moments.

God is acquainted with all my ways; therefore, nothing can hinder the fulfillment of my purpose. Even when I did not understand His plan, He chose to love me. I am a testament to His healing power and beauty. Today, I share my story to be a hope to others, not because I have arrived but because as I take one step at a time in my journey, holding on to the hope of my salvation, God is continually expanding my story to speak of His grace and blessings. I am blessed with a pure sense of joy and happiness because I know He will always lead me exactly to where I need to be.

REFLECTIONS

My goal in life is to magnify God by sharing the story He wrote through me to encourage and motivate the little girl, the young lady, the friend, the mentee, and the mother figure, as well as my single, engaged, and married sisters to push through life with joy and the hope of obtaining excellent worship unto God. The power of God is an amazing tool that, as people, we are blessed with. If you don't know the Lord, it is my prayer and heartfelt desire that the journey that I was blessed to take, the road I have been assigned to travel, and the experience I gained in my life will be a change agent to your greatness in life.

To truly experience greatness and shine for the world to see, God must be the center of your being. This is my challenge to you.

"That if you confess with your mouth the Lord Jesus and believe in your heart that God has raised Him from the dead, you will be saved. For with the heart one believes unto righteousness, and with the mouth, confession is made unto salvation."

Romans:10:9-10

"For whoever calls on the name of the Lord shall be saved."

Romans:10:13

THOUGHTS FOR YOUR JOURNEY

God has given each one of us the ability to shine so others can see. Our life should always reflect God's sacrifice and brokenness for us. What have you gone through that you can use to be a ministry? Please know, somebody is depending on your light to see.

Remember, no matter what you face, if God is part of the equation, it's bound to have a positive outcome with a reward on this earth as well as in the heavens. I was broken to shine so the world could see the light of God through my life

"Let your light shine before men, that they may see your good works and glorify your Father in heaven."

Matthew 5:16

Twenty-fifth wedding anniversary vow renewal and our 50th birthday celebration
Ethiopian style in memory of Dad

Cheers to life and love

StoryTerrace

Made in the USA
Columbia, SC
18 January 2023